My Open Heart

Stories & Essays by Members of SEIU Healthcare 1199NE

Sponsored by the 1199 New England Training & Upgrading Fund

HARDBALL

PRESS

Edited By Tim Sheard

My Open Heart – 1199 Nursing Home and Homecare Workers
Tell Their Story
Edited by Timothy Sheard

Published by Hard Ball Press.
Information available at: www.hardballpress.com
ISBN-13:
978-1717290694
ISBN-10:
1717290698
Cover art by Tim Sheard & D. Bass
Book design and format by D. Bass

Library of Congress Cataloging-in-Publication Data
Sheard, Timothy
Caring – Nursing Home Workers Tell Their Story
1. Nursing Homes 2. Certified Nursing Assistant (CNA). 3. 1199
4. Health Care Unions.

This collection of stories is dedicated to the nursing home residents, rehab patients, homecare clients, and their families who rely on us for their care. We love and honor them, and we wish for them to continue living their lives to the fullest, and to experience peaceful days and restful nights.

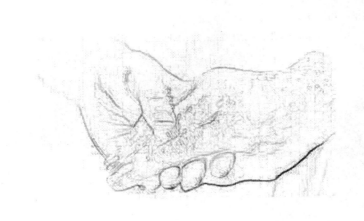

CONTENTS

*Some of the Writers of Expressions of Joy
with their instructor*

Book One

Expressions of Joy

A collection of writings from the 1199 Training Fund Summer 2016 Creative Writing Class

Introduction

Everyone has a story to tell. Through compassionate, student-centered guidance, students of the 1199 Training Fund's Summer 2016 Creative Writing Class were able to explore personal moments of their greatest joy and discover strategies and techniques to craft their most cherished and compelling stories of joy. I am pleased to present this collection of creative writings authored by these students.

This writing course focused on creating a vivid and memorable account of each student's most joyous moment. Beyond the academics of creating a well-organized, creative writing piece using the full writing process, students concentrated on the refinement of vocabulary and use of figurative language. They expanded their ability to access their emotional side and awakened their senses to explore their emotions through language.

The authors of these very remarkable essays truly allow the reader to understand, see, feel, and be part of their distinctive, joyful moment. Please take a moment and share in their expressions of joy!

Alma Farnsworth,
1199 Training Fund Instructor, Summer, 2016

very cordial; however, he did not make it easy for me, implying that he did not view me as an ideal candidate because of my age and lack of work experience. However, he decided he would give me an opportunity to work for their company starting with a 6-month probation period to prove my worth. This I did successfully. Although I was never praised or told my portfolio was being reviewed, I felt that I was meeting and exceeding the company's targets, and increasing and maintaining their existing customer base and generating good revenue.

Approximately one year on the job, while I was peacefully enjoying breakfast in the staff kitchen, my director, the owner's son, walked in and asked me to meet with him in his office. At first, I was nervous and scared because he was very meticulous and would chastise anyone for incompetence, but while I was walking to his office, I remembered he was no[t] in his usual serious demeanor. It helped to quell my fears a bit, but not completely.

The 40 foot walk felt like 400. Finally, I got to his office, and he inquired about how I was doing. He asked how I was enjoying working for the company and if I planned to stay with them for a while. Of course, I answered with high praise for the company and my work experience there. He then looked directly at me smiling, and said, "We really appreciate you and would like to give you a raise. How much would you like?" I was caught off guard and surprised to hear these words flowing from his mouth. Dizzily, I responded with a nominal figure of maybe a 10% increase for the year. He looked at me and smiled saying, "No, you deserve more because our Miami office really loves you, and you are doing a fantastic job; how about 30%?"

With a questioning gesture, he asked, "How about 30%?" I stared at him in disbelief; I was smiling and trembling, yet paralyzed with joy. Although it felt like minutes, I stood there for a few seconds just staring and smiling, not saying a word. He then proudly smiled at me and said, "You really deserve it! You've done a fantastic job increasing sales and our clientele, and we really want you to be happy; keep up the good work."

The only response I could muster was to whisper "Thank You" as I was lost for words. I think that the sound of my heart beating like an African drum in my chest was louder than my soft words "thank you".

quietly, I said "thank you" again, and smiling like a kid in a candy store, I slowly walked back to my desk. I tried my best to conceal the good news and emotions from the rest of the office staff as I did not want my coworkers to be envious of me or become aware of what just transpired in my manager's office. Quietly, I sat at my desk for a few minutes trying with every fiber in my body to overcome, appreciate, and understand what felt like an out-of-body experience.

I thanked God for finally allowing me to receive my raise and recognition and for allowing me to finally feel appreciated and vindicated. I was ready to continue on my quest to prove that age does not matter, and short skirts and long flowing hair do not get the job done!

Anna Farnsworth
Sophomore in High School
(Alma's granddaughter)

"Oink, Oink"

As I limped toward the judge, I could taste the victory of my second place success. Even having a broken left foot at that time would not stop me from showing my pig, Carmella.

From all the different pigs and showmen, I had just received second place in the Senior Fitting and Showmanship class (ages 15-21). On this date, October 1, 2015 at the Big E fairgrounds, I earned a higher status in my showmanship division because I had just turned 15-years-old that day, and I needed to show with all the advanced senior showmen.

From this promotion, I became more confident in myself. I was then upgraded in more competitive divisions of showing pigs for my age group. At this show, just turning 15 on the show date made me the youngest showman in this division. From this opportunity, I have increased my showmanship skills and gained more respect from the other showmen around the show circuit. From here on, people knew me and they needed to watch out for Anna Farnsworth because from now on I knew I was going to become better and better.

Placing second in the large class of advanced showmen proved to me that after all my hard work, it had paid off with prize money and personal victory. This made me feel on top of the world.

Being involved in this hobby over the years has made me love and want to pursue my dream of being more successful in the swine business. I love to show pigs because it is very entertaining and each pig has its own personality and is extremely intelligent. Their intelligence makes it easy to teach them new showmanship moves. Also, I get to have fun socially with all the other show people. I meet new people from all over the East Coast and have more opportunities open for me.

Showing pigs takes patience and great multitasking skills. This hobby teaches me many skills, responsibility, social skills, and importantly, leadership. I would not trade this hobby for any other sport.

To start off each show season, I go up to Warren, Massachusetts to Hill Top Hog Farm to choose any number of pigs that were a month old. There are many breeds of pigs that I can choose from, such as a Duroc, Berkshire, or Hampshire, but my favorite breed is the Hampshire crossbred pigs because this breed develops a bigger built body. Fred Spain (the owner of the farm) is an extraordinary pig breeder, who would make sure I have the best pigs that my money could buy.

I kept my pigs at the Bowman family farm in Tolland, Connecticut. I was friends with his two girls, who were just a bit younger than me. Without having a close relationship with the Bowman family, I would have never had the opportunity to open my eyes to do more in the different departments of agriculture. They have shared their special secrets of showing and picking the great quality pigs from Hill Top Farm. Knowing the Bowmans for six plus years, they are like a second family to me. They have helped me to become a better showman, supported me, and helped me learn how to show pigs; it all started because of them.

Because of this family, I started at a 1-class local show, going on to gain the opportunity to show at the biggest show in New England. Each year, I gain remarkable knowledge about pigs from the other contestants, but mostly from the Clum and Perrizattie family. Over the years of showing and seeing them at the shows, I have made a great bond with those families. From the first year showing around the states with these families, I have learned many skills from their comments.

At the Bowman farm, we have changed and improved the living conditions of the pigs' housing by upgrading and increasing the amount of land on which the pigs can run free. We have structured a better feeding program and diet for the pigs and increased the cleaning products we put on them.

This made me feel proud of what I learned and how I take care of the animals. At Fred's farm, he has upgraded his breeding program to produce higher quality pigs.

During last year's show season (2015), I only chose one pig, Carmella. From there, I had just committed myself to take care of and teach her how to become an outstanding showmanship pig until it was time to use her for meat at the end of show season. A quote from Mike Clum that will stay with me is, "Showing pigs is a sport; they are the athletes and you are the coach. So, how much effort you put into the athlete is the quality of effort the pig will show." This means so much to me because many people do not consider this a sport. I take great pride in showing and keeping my pigs in a clean and healthy environment.

Throughout the six months of having Carmella, I had created a bond with her, her trust and respect me as a trainer. My feelings of working with her have given me frustration when she would run away from me, but a relaxing feeling when she returned when she wanted to go to sleep. Knowing that pigs are very intelligent made it easier for me to teach Carmella how to walk slowly next to me, and I taught her to listen to my voice with the show stick to create a better way for her to move around the show pen.

I had put as much as I could into this animal to create a great show pig. With trying to handle her, school, different activities, and appointments, I challenged myself to make more time to work with her. As the six months went by, I went to six different marvelous shows, leading up to the moment of my success at the Big E Pig Show. Those six months have called for waking up early in the morning to feed and going every weekend to a different show. I now understand that not everything comes easy; we all must put in effort to achieve success.

Remembering my class at The Big E, I felt a feeling of joy and accomplishment. When I was finishing limping around the show pen, all I could see through my foggy, oily eyes was the great audience cheerin[g] me on for my victory. After I retrieved my pig from the show pen, I had bent down to pet my enjoyable, oiled-up pig to notify her that we have gotten a great placing and that we have just finished up our class. As we were waiting to be dismissed from the class, all I could taste was the nasty, salty sweat running down my face entering my dry, cracked lips.

Anna Farnsworth and Fred Spain
Victories of Showing Anna's Pigs
Terryville Country Fair, 2016

Finally after getting Carmella back to the stall, I got to clean up and watch a video of the exciting class that I have just finished. As I watched the video, I noticed that my pig had peed in my boot. That was e reason why I kept on smelling something sour, and I kept on hearing a sloshing sound when my right boot stepped on the ground. That did not matter to me. I was proud of Carmella and felt great joy with my outstanding second place win!

From traveling to each show and gaining experience, I have challenged myself to compete at the top shows for pigs with Carmella. Receiving amazing placings and earning about $650 in prize money in 2015, I can now consider myself becoming an accomplished showman--one of the best.

From my experience, I have gained motivation and focus on what matters to me. I have learned to acknowledge and work hard for my hopes of tomorrow. As I grow, I will become a good role model, teaching other showmen the great secrets of showing pigs just like the Clum and Perrizattie family are doing for me now.

NEW ENGLAND HEALTH CARE EMPLOYEES UNION

DISTRICT 1199

AND THE CONNECTICUT NURSING HOMES

T&U

TRAINING & UPGRADING

FUND

Allison Jones
Fresh River Healthcare, East Windsor
(Allison Jones with sons)

The Walk

In 1982 when I was sixteen, I was a mother, or as I once overheard someone in the welfare office state, "a statistic." Her facial expressions led me to believe that it wasn't anything nice and that I should have been embarrassed and ashamed in some way. In 1994, the Welfare Reform Bill was signed. The Bill was an attempt to educate and train individuals who were receiving welfare so that they would be skilled enough to find jobs and gain independence. The program's main requirement stated: recipients must be enrolled in a work or educational program within a specific time frame or his or her cash benefits would be cut.

Nine young single mothers, including me, in the community, read our letters, and all of us reacted in fear and panic. We came to a conclusion and agreed to enroll in night classes at Hartford High School to ensure we continued receiving our benefits before the deadline.

I remember the enrollment day as if it was yesterday. When I met the counselor assigned to my case, she gazed at me with the same expression as the social worker, who referred to me as a 'statistic'. She forcefully made a remark to me as I sat across from her that day. "You don't have many credits."

I felt a lump in my throat as I held back tears. I

remember feeling light headed and a full body crippling. I felt defeated before I even began. Although I dropped out of school in the ninth grade, my school counselor reassured me that this wasn't a reason to feel overcome. I remember her reassuring tone as she told me that I'd just have to begin with foundation courses. It was her smile that gave me hope. I felt as though I had been freed from a rock that had been sitting on my chest since the moment I received that letter.

The first step for me was to enroll in night classes; the next step began the day the nine of us girls met in front of the school. During our walks home together, we would discuss our classes. Most of the girls were taking classes together. I, on the other hand, began with fewer credits, which in a way deemed me less advanced than the others. I felt defeated and that they had more of an advantage than I. But, with my tenacity, I had hope.

That first night when I arrived home from school, I sat at the kitchen table. I reached into my backpack and retrieved my schedule, and I must have glanced over each sentence that I wrote in my schedule a thousand times. Doubting myself a thousand more, I had a talk with myself that night and came to the realization that if I was going to conquer the world, I first must conquer my fear. I also came to understand that fear is never a positive solution to any problem. I made it through that first day.

I laid my head on my pillow and closed my eyes. As my mind drifted off into a deep meditation, I received a visit from my old friend fear. Sitting in the dark corner of my mind, this friend would whisper to me all the bad things that could happen. I did not give in and put this out of mind for now. I finally fell asleep.

The first week of classes started off great! The nine of us girls walked an average of 1.8 miles to and from the school. We made this walk five days a week. Each night as we walked home, our laughing and telling stories made the distance and time feel as if it was just a walk around the corner. But sadly enough as the weeks continued, girls would disappear one by one. Until one evening, the last girl told me she was going to drop out, too.

Fear came rushing over me like a black cloud of devastation, which devoured all the hope I had left. I felt overwhelming sadness and depression. I told myself, "You are not going to be another statistic."

I repeated this over and over, and this became my only reasoning, my motivation, my weapon. So, I continued the walks alone and slowly it became a daily routine for me.

One night during my walk home, I met a new friend, a tall, well-groomed gentleman who was out walking his dog, which was a beautiful black lab. Our conversation began with hello and an inquiry about the backpack I was carrying over my shoulder. We walked for two blocks, asking one another questions. We'd go back and forth as if we were on an episode of Jeopardy. Before turning around, he would pop a mint. Maybe it was to cover the cigarette smell. Whatever the case may have been, he was always polite and courteous, and I never felt as though he judged me. From then on, with time passing like clockwork, the tall man and I would walk and exchange stories.

For the upcoming semester, I was told there would be morning classes offered on Washington Street. I had to know if I would be eligible to enroll in night and morning classes. Once I received the okay, I went on and registered for morning and evening courses. One of the courses required for me to successfully complete was a keyboarding course, which was only offered in the mornings.

After conquering the registration issue, the next barrier that stood in my way was the fact that the course was filled and no new registrations were being accepted. I did not wish for anyone to drop out; however, I knew that if the others did not understand fear like I understood fear, they would eventually give into its demands.

While waiting for a spot to open, I asked if I could sit in the back of the room with my typewriter (that I went out and purchased from the Salvation Army) until a slot opened up. I argued my case until finally my request was granted. In less than a week, I had a spot in the keyboarding class. No more lugging my hardcover, powder blue, incased typewriter on the bus two days a week.

As weeks passed, I noticed I had not seen my older friend and his dog. Maybe he went on vacation I thought to myself. I hope I didn't say anything to offend him the last time we had a chat. A month before graduation, I noticed a younger man, who favored the older gentleman, walking the black lab. In pure excitement, I yelled out the dog's name. He raced toward me pulling the young man along the way. "Where's the owner, the older man?" I asked. "Unfortunately, my father passed away from a heart attack. And you are?" the stranger replied. I was devastated. I explained to the young man that in rain or snow his father and I would walk the dimly lit two blocks each evening after I left classes keeping one another company along the way.

Finally, the last day of night class, I took my last walk and spoke out loud as if my friend was there talking back to me. Everyone along the way has moved on or passed away, and now on this final walk, I walked alone. "Well, this is the last walk my friend. This part of my journey is coming to an end. Thank you for your kind words, your support, and for being a beacon in the dark on those nights I walked down the poorly lit street. Carrying only my backpack filled with my hopes, my dreams, and determination, I thank you."

As my story concludes, I'd like to share a quote by David Brinley, who states, "A successful man is one who can lay a firm foundation with the bricks that others have thrown at him or her." A program that would have taken the average individual four years to achieve had only taken me two.

I was considered by the State of Connecticut and U.S. Government a 'statistic'; however, I used each brick to lay a foundation. This foundation helped me to achieve a diploma and certification in the healthcare field as a Certified Nursing Assistant and Phlebotomist. I soon secured a career in the work force, and I am working toward earning my college degree.

Each night after school, I would help my three children with their homework. After completing the lessons, I would tell them a story with a message. I would ask my children what was the moral of each story?

As I write these words for this essay, I ask myself a similar question. To me, my story explains a simple lesson that there would be times in life when you must walk alone with just your determination and the faith within yourself. You should not give into fear by quitting, dropping out, or giving up. As you lay stones, they become roads, and roads become journeys. Through your journeys, you can reach your destination.

My children grew up to become fine young adults. Each one has created a path of their own by laying their own foundations.

Not every path one takes will be smooth and clearly paved. It is sometimes lonely and rough, discouraging and tempting. But, remember one day your road could split the same as mine. One day your children will start on their path, so create a firm foundation with a good example, and you'll never know how far the road could take them.

I'm on the left, a proud mother of my sons. Antwan is standing in the middle and Charles is on the right.

My Graduation Day, the day I received my high school diploma! The two children are my two youngest, Willie (6-years-old) and Antwan (5-years-old); the lady in the white is my mother, and to the right are my brother and aunt. Antwan in his graduation attire: "Antwan Jones of Enfield sends a message to his mom from his seat among the graduates Friday at Asnuntuck Community College in Enfield."

Ricky Lewis Maldonado
West Hartford Health and Rehabilitation Center

Vacation in Puerto Rico

On early Mother's Day 2016, my family and I received tragic news. My oldest and only brother, Luis Alexander Maldonado, was killed in a hit and run car accident. It was one of the most difficult things I have ever been through. Before my brother was killed, my mother and stepdad had planned a vacation for a getaway to Puerto Rico, where my family was born and raised, and I was going to stay home to watch over the house. Mom being 'mom' insisted I go with them since I have never been there before. She always talked about bringing my brother and me to Puerto Rico. It had been four months since he had been gone, so I immediately booked a flight to go to Puerto Rico with them because the thought of being alone didn't settle well with me or my relatives.

Ricky with his brother

As the two weeks flew by for me to depart on my vacation, my nerves and imagination were getting the best of me. I was scared, nervous, and anxious about finally stepping foot on this beautiful island. I was altogether a mess.

I have always been told by family, who were raised in Puerto Rico, regarding how majestic the island would be. I was totally numb and silent as a mouse because I was in suspense knowing that in six hours I would finally be in Puerto Rico. As we started heading to Bradley International Airport, I was not one bit tired by waking up at 3:30 a.m. I was ready to leave Hartford, Connecticut.

My family and I arrived at Bradley International Airport at 5:30 a.m. Now, I was feeling drained from getting very little sleep. Going through what felt like an obstacle course to get through security, we finally sat and all had a bite to eat. Then, we realized that we should be at our gate early enough to make sure we didn't miss our flight. While boarding, I felt goose bumps all over me because it had been almost 14 years since I boarded a plane. We found our seats, which were very close to each other. This was a relief to me, but I was still hesitant about flying. The plane taxiing for takeoff made my stomach turn as if I was going to hurl. I put my hands together and prayed. I noticed a woman next to me, who was doing the same, and we smiled. Within the four hours heading to my destination, I finally dozed off, while looking out the window.

Waking up to the flight attendant's announcement that the plane had landed, I literally wanted to run and just leave my bag on the plane. It was really hard trying to wait as people took their time exiting the plane. Full of excitement, I rushed to catch my first glimpse of my parents' homeland.

When I finally got close enough to the door to peak out, the scenery was spectacular. First things that caught my eyes were giant palm trees swaying side to side and birds of all colors and sizes flying around. I smelled Spanish spices from restaurants around the airport. There were no words to express how I felt at that time because it was all so new to me.

As my family and I waited for our cousins to come pick us up, I was still in awe, slowly realizing I had finally made it to Puerto Rico. As I heard a loud beep, the adventure began. It's been a while since my cousins and I reunited; off we went. There was so much to catch up on as we talked and joked about it being my first time in Puerto Rico. There was so much to do. While driving through the streets, I noticed the road became tighter and tighter as if it was made for a one way street. I glanced to my right, and noticed the road was bordered by cliffs. It was like a scary rollercoaster, but my cousins were so used to driving through these roads that it was a piece of cake to them. The color of the houses were pink, yellow, blue, and all different colors. People were outside hosing down their outdoor porches or hanging their clothes on the outside bars. It was a beautiful thing to see people without washers or dryers and doing things by hand.

It was very hard to sleep that first night at my cousins' home. One reason was because of the native frogs called a coqui, which are only found in Puerto Rico. They are the small frogs that compete with each other making sounds by going back and forth. In the mornings, I always woke up to the roosters' cock-a-doodle doo; it was the worst noise ever. When going outside, there was nothing more beautiful than seeing the mountains surrounding the city. The neighbors raised farm animals such as bulls, cows, chickens, roosters, and sheep that just roamed the fields. My love for animals kept me outside late at night and sometimes early mornings just watching them, while drinking my coffee.

Cabo Rojo Beach

As far as the weather, it rained the first few days, but after that, it was hot, but always breezy. One day, my cousins and I headed out to Cabo Rojo Beach. It is one of the most beautiful beaches I have ever seen. The water was as crystal clear as my mom used to tell me and not very cold.

One time while floating in the water, I closed my eyes and thanked God for this moment, and I wished my brother was here because that's what my mom wanted for us. We stayed in Puerto Rico for two weeks, and it was an incredible trip for us to share together as a family. Going through this horrific tragedy of my brother's death, this trip brought all of us closer than ever. This is something that my brother would have wanted. It makes me realize that family is everything, and that's why this was one of my most joyous moments because I knew he was with us in spirit. This experience also showed me that through the bumps in life, anyone can still keep moving.

Just don't give up hope.

Donna Monteith
Touchpoints at Farmington

The Day I Passed My LPN Entrance Exam

I walked into E. C. Goodwin Technical High School in New Britain to take an LPN entrance test. I entered a huge auditorium filled with a rainbow of faces, both male and female. I was so nervous my knees were shaking like leaves in the wind. A lady with a bright green blouse and big bushy brows came over towards me and handed me some pencils and told me to have a seat.

I looked around, and everyone else looked just as nervous. I made my way to the top right-hand corner of the auditorium and sat down. The guy next to me began fidgeting with his pencils, tapping his feet, and popping his gum. It was so distracting. I looked at him and gave him the evil eye; immediately he stopped.

The lady with the bright green blouse went up and down each aisle dropping off papers. I hurriedly grabbed my papers to look them over before we started, but all I saw were bubbles and numbers.

Someone yelled over the intercom, "We will now be starting the test." I looked at the test and became perplexed. I thought to myself, "Oh my, so many questions." I put my head down and ignored all the people around me. I started taking the test. Halfway through, I became sleepy and started dozing off.

When the test was over, I got up thinking, "Boy, this test was hard."

I didn't think anything about it until a couple of weeks later. The administrators from the Nursing Program called to tell me that my test results were in, and they would like to set up an interview. I was surprised, but I was worried at the same time.

Getting that wonderful news, I went to T. J. Maxx and bought myself a new outfit, more on the conservative side. I bought black pants, a black blazer, a white shirt, and some accessories to match. I felt great, and I was feeling optimistic.

I went for the interview at E.C. Goodwin Tech. The administrator sat me down and said, "Congratulations, you passed the test." I almost fainted. I was so excited because getting an interview sounded promising. I said, "Oh my God, little old me; I did it!" It brought tears to my eyes.

The next day, I couldn't wait to get to work to tell my co-workers about my wonderful news. I saw one of the aides who took the test before and did not pass. I showed her my results. You should have seen her face. She exclaimed, "As much as you love to party, I didn't think you would have passed."

She went and got a couple more aides and told them the story. They all gathered around to look at my results. About three to four of the aides took the test and did not pass. I think my co-workers were just jealous.

I had a feeling of pure jubilation. Passing the exam made me feel even smarter. It goes to show you, whatever you put your mind to, you can achieve.

Maribel Rodriguez
Autumn Lake Healthcare at Bucks Hill, Waterbury

Memories

It was May 13, 2016 when I was on vacation in Las Vegas, Nevada with my sister and best friend. We had a great week and our vacation was coming to end, but there was one more day left, and we had to go to the Grand Canyon. We bought our tickets the night before. Our great adventure would start at 7:00 in the morning. It would take about four hours to get there, and we made a stop at Hoover Dam and a few other places. Finally, we arrived.

When I arrived, I could not contain my excitement. The sky was a majestic blue with white clouds floating by like cotton. The sun was gleaming over us like rays of gold. As we walked down to the viewing area, a gentle breeze brushed across my face as I breathed in the fresh air. I stood in awe of this magnificent moment.

The amazing view was breathtaking. We saw majestic mountains of sandstone with hues of orange and reddish tones with peaks and valleys – so glorious. The dimensions and magnitude were so impressive. I was elated and felt as if I was in a different world. Pictures of the Grand Canyon are spectacular; however, nothing can prepare you for the majesty and grandeur of the Grand Canyon.

It's an experience you can feel and see only in person. I dream of a time when I can return and spend more time exploring and reflecting on its beauty.

A View from Above the Grand Canyon
Maribel Rodriguez

This majestic piece of paradise is awe inspiring.
Its azure skies have floating cotton clouds
so ever gently floating over these amazing
peaks of purple hues, reddish tones
and shimmers of gold.

The valleys and crevices are so deep
That my eyes wish to see every single piece
of this glorious land.

I reached the bottom,
where my eyes gloss over blue waters
with shades of glorious green
and ripples flowing by.

When I think I saw all the beauty
that this place has to offer,
I caught a glimpse of emerald bushes
and trees growing graciously
from the sides of the regal mountains—
A feast for my eyes and soul to see.

Dee Seegobin
Chelsea Place, Hartford

My Most Joyous Moment:
My First Job

As I recall, I was 17-years old, and I was reading the employment ads when I noticed that a dentist needed people to train as dental hygienists. I asked my friend to take me to the dentist's office. When my friend read the ad, he said, "No way is that dentist going to hire you." I asked him why he came to that conclusion; he said, "Because the dentist needs people who have a college degree." I told my friend that although I don't have a college degree, I will still go to speak to the dentist. So, my friend took me to the dentist's office.

When we reached the dentist's office, I was amazed to see that so many people were there. I filled out the application, but I was as nervous as a cat because I had never filled out an application before. In the application, it asked how much money you wanted to earn during training. I wrote on the paper "It didn't matter." It also asked how much money you needed to earn after training, and I wrote, "According to the quality of my work."

My friend told me to forget about that job, but I ignored him. In the back of my head, I kept telling myself that I started this, and I am still going to apply. By him saying that, I felt that he thought that I was not qualified enough for the position.

To my surprise, I received a letter for an interview. I showed the letter to my friend. Surprisingly, he said, "You got a reply?" By the expression on his face, I could tell he didn't believe it. I was so overjoyed. I couldn't wait to go for the interview. Receiving this letter made me jump for joy.

On the day of the interview, I was very nervous. As I was approaching the waiting room, I noticed about twelve girls sitting there. When I saw so many girls, I thought to myself, "Maybe I should leave." But an inner voice kept telling me to stay. As the dentist kept calling the interviewers one at a time, one of the girls whispered to me that she noticed every time the dentist came to get one of the girls, he kept looking at me. For some reason, I wasn't paying any attention to her. All I know I was like a little puppy, scared to death. All I was thinking was that I am sitting here with these college graduates. I was here sitting beside them, and I had not started college. It was as if I was a little lamb surrounded by these giant elephants.

When the dentist came and called my name, I knew I was shaking and trembling like a leaf. He stretched his hand out and said, "I am Doctor David Thomas." I smiled, shook his hand, and said my name. At the same time, I noticed he was good looking and neatly dressed; he had on a white lab coat, and his hair was neatly combed. He told me to follow him, and we went into a small office. He pointed to a chair and told me to sit.

As I was sitting, I noticed him sitting, still looking at the application in his hand. He looked up and asked me why I applied for this position. I felt nervous about answering his question. Then, this inner voice in me was saying to be brave. I straightened myself and answered, "I needed a job, and I would like to learn how to be a good hygienist."

He looked at me and said, "What if I tell you I wanted to give you a chance in learning?" I looked at him with my hands locked together. My heart was racing, and within my inner self, I was wondering if he meant that he is going to hire me. "Was he telling me that he is hiring me?"

Then, what I really wanted to hear came out of his mouth. He said, "Can you start on Monday?" At that moment, I thought I was frozen. I then said, "Oh, yes." I know for a fact that I was stammering. That was the most joyous moment of my life. I had a job, my first paying job.

I went and told my friend that I was going to start my training on Monday. My friend said, "What?" From the look on his face, I knew that he was shocked. "You mean to tell me, all those people who were there and the dentist hired you?" I said, "Yes!" and I was giggling like a child. I couldn't wait for Monday.

Monday morning came, and I wore my white dress and white pair of shoes; I was as happy as a lark. When I arrived at the office, the dentist greeted me and introduced me to another girl, and he said that he was going to train the two of us.

Later in the week, the dentist told me he had over two hundred applicants, and he chose this girl with a college degree, and me, who didn't have a college degree. As time went on, I learned each of the instruments, and I also helped him to make dentures.

> *"Commonsense is a flower*
> *that doesn't grow in*
> *everyone's garden." To me*
> *what he meant was that*
> *what your hands can do,*
> *sometimes education can't*
> *do. He also said that he*
> *took a risk hiring me, and*
> *he had no regrets."*

One day, he called me into his office, and told me that he is giving me a raise of salary, and I must keep it to myself. I asked him, " Why?" He said that I was learning and doing more than the other girl.

He also said, "Commonsense is a flower that doesn't grow in everyone's garden." To me what he meant was that what your hands can do, sometimes education can't do. He also said that he took a risk hiring me, and he had no regrets.

Two years later, I got married to my friend, whom I mentioned in this story. On the third year, I got pregnant and was very sick. So I had to leave the job. The job was a great experience. I was very determined. There is a saying 'when you listen to your heart, it will lead you where you belong'.

And, my determination led me to a joyous moment.

Steve Thornton with Shoeleather writers

BOOK TWO

STORIES INSPIRED BY THE SHOELEATHER WALKING TOUR

Steve Thornton

The following stories were written in summer 2017 by 1199 members as part of the Training Fund's creative writing class. On the first night of class, they took a shoeleather walking tour of Hartford, led by retired 1199 Vice President Steve Thornton.

Introduction

The 1199 Training and Upgrading Fund did not just "appear" in the nursing home contracts that workers negotiate with their employers. The Fund was, and still is, the product of a very real struggle between the healthcare workers and owners.

In the 1980s, it took a strike of hundreds of Connecticut 1199ers that forced employers to join and contribute to the 1199 Training Fund. The writers in this book have all benefited from that first sacrifice.

They understand this. The stories they have written reflect their first-hand knowledge about what it means to struggle. Even if the incidents took place a century ago or an ocean away, our Union's members can link their own lives to these far-away battles.

In order to read the word, they have learned to read the world. There is no greater compliment I could give to them and their teachers.

Steve Thornton

Denise Dickinson
Fresh River Healthcare, East Windsor

To Doug & Mara
I am proud to
be a member of
1199 Nursing Union
r in Healthcare,
Love.
Denise

50

Rabbi Abraham Feldman: A Voice of the Community

My intent for signing up for the creative writing class was to learn the skill of writing in an enthusiastic and fun method, to catch the reader's mind and heart, and to use new knowledge for improving the quality of my written work.

The creative writing class took a tour of parts of Hartford called the Shoeleather Walking Tour, which was given by Steve Thornton, an historian. Steve Thornton is a native of Hartford, and he has dedicated his whole adult life as an activist in Harford. He teaches people about the city's landmarks and its citizens' past. I am inspired by his innovative and industrious insight regarding the roots of our capitol city of Hartford. He has worked with Hartford-based health care workers, New England District 1199 Union, and campaigns and organizations for over 40 years. I am grateful and enthused to learn about historical backgrounds of Hartford through his Shoeleather Walking Tour. His stories about people of Hartford made me want to push for opportunities in my life, work, community, and union.

Steve Thornton talked about Rabbi Abraham Feldman's accomplishments and how, through his highly regarded work and career, he was a legend of Hartford. From Steve Thornton's story about Rabbi

Feldman, I was overtaken by his remarks and wanted to do more research.

Rabbi Feldman was born in 1893 and died in 1977. His birthplace was Kiev, Ukraine, and he moved to the East Side of Manhattan, New York City ("A Finding Aid"). He was "nationally known as a Jewish leader and an ecumenist", a respected Rabbi of Beth Israel synagogue, and for his involvement in community affairs (Flint). His voice made a difference in citizens' moral issues, which he took to heart, and he was sympathetic to their concerns. He was a strong leader for civil and human rights and social justice, which echoed what people believed in regarding their community. Steve Thornton talked about how Rabbi Feldman stood up for civil rights for all people, including Catholics, and he fought against the death penalty. I agree with the Rabbi's outspokenness against the death penalty. In other words, two wrongs don't make a right. In addition, he supported the Hartford Food Share Program, Connecticut Birth Control League, and Hartford Music Foundation ("A Finding Aid"). He was also a member and founder of Connecticut Advisory Committee of the U.S. Commission on Civil Rights and the Hartford Rotary Club (Mindell).

From reading about Rabbi Feldman, I feel knowing what matters to your neighbors helps in making a difference to create a healthier atmosphere to a well-rounded city or town. For example, I personally share Rabbi Feldman's controversial ideals in helping women receive proper birth control access instead of them bringing children into the world before they are physically and mentally prepared to bring up a child. The Birth Control Federation of America has done tremendous work such as "distribut[ing] contraceptive information to clinics, conducting laboratory and clinical research in contraceptive methods primarily through the Birth Control Clinical Research Bureau (BCCRB), support[ing] state committees and leagues, and promot[ing] the inclusion of courses on contraceptive techniques in medical school curricula" ("Birth Control Organizations").

The Rabbi's roads of leadership had many avenues that advanced around the world for peace and equality. Rabbi Feldman encouraged citizens of communities to be open-minded about their rights. He was vice-president of World Union Progressive Judaism during 1947- 1949 ("A Finding Aid"). He provided a place of worship at Beth Temple sanctuary for a group of displaced worshipers, who were of non-Jewish faith. By moving away from traditions, he would not permit worshippers to wear a yarmulke or tallis (Mindell). For instance, when a conservative man wished to wear a yarmulke to marry, being his right for an old Jewish custom, the Rabbi would not agree (Mindell). The Beth Israel congregation was the first congregation to embrace the new arrivals of Soviet Jews to America (Mindell). In my mind, he was an ambitious activist for what he believed in, which inspires me to be stand up for what I want believe in and want to actively pursue.

I am a proud member of the 1199 Union for 11 years

now, and its history is important to me. The Union was built on the foundation of Martin Luther King's concepts of social justice, and the Union led strikes for actual benefits concerning health care. Sparks hit the sky in 1958 when King organized hospital workers to fight for security, overtime pay, and minimum wage ("1199 History"). King said, "More than a fight for union rights, a fight for dignity." The health care workers were breaking their backs and doing difficult and harsh work taking care of patients and "making only 80 cents ($6.00/hr today)" ("1199 History"). This is peanuts in today's view! I would be unable to have a home or would starve or would not have clothes if it was not for the years of struggle of my 1199 Union.

Throughout my life and from working for iCare Management, I have learned that I can't be speechless if I want to make a difference or to improve my personal life, my job opportunities, and my community for my niece's and nephew's futures. To make a difference, for one example, I marched in the spring of 2017 at the capitol and talked to devoted legislators for increasing the smoking age from 18 to 21. The legislators are still sifting through intense discussions on the bill to raise the smoking age.

I totally realize that your attitude pertains to how you view the world and your personal decisions. At 57-years-old, I am faced with daily dilemmas that involve making simple to more difficult decisions. The key to successful resolutions is a positive and confident outlook. I know that 'where there is a will, there is a way'. Steve Thornton, Rabbi Feldman, and Martin L King, all had positive, productive, and important leadership roles to create a difference in people's personal civil rights even today. It is vital that people understand and get along with diverse cultures, and that they can choose their own religion. With current contract debates, I totally understand how workers and management have to argue views on health care benefits and human rights, which honor and stabilize our lives to achieve prosperous careers and productive lifestyles. I believe we walk with a cross for our civil rights like Jesus walked with a cross to die for our sins!

I am blessed that I had a delightful middle-class upbringing in a suburb of our great capitol. I am determined and excited to continue my interest in community and national affairs. I am inspired by Rabbi Feldman to continue with the 1199 Union pursuits, to be an active member of the AARP, a committee member of the Relay for Life, as well as walking for Alzheimer's and Relay for Life to raise funds for the world-wide organization's research.

I am pleased with our 1199 Union's Pension Fund for retirement and Training Fund, which allowed me to take this writing class. These classes are essential to me. I am going to uphold previous leaders' outstanding work, and I am looking forward to building on their accomplishments.

Works Cited

"A Finding Aid to the Abraham J. Feldman Papers. 1913-1977 (bulk 1930-1970)." American Jewish Archives. 1979, collections.americanjewisharchives.org/ms/ms0038/ms0038.html. Collections.americanjewishachives.org. Accessed 10 Aug 2107.

"Birth Control Organizations." New York University. New York University, nyu.edu/projects/sanger/aboutms/organization_bcfa.php. Accessed 18 Aug 2017.

Flint, Peter. "Abraham Feldman, Jewish Leader, Dies." New York Times. The New York Times Company, 1977, nytimes.com/1977/07/23/archives/abraham-feldman-jewish-leader-dies-nationally-known-as-an-ecumenist.html. Accessed 18 Aug 2017.

Mindell, Cindy. "Congregation Beth Israel at 170–West Hartford synagogue marks a milestone anniversary." Connecticut Jewish Ledger, Judie Jacobson, 2013, jewishledger.com/2013/05/congregation-beth-israel-at-170-west-hartford-synagogue-marks-a-milestone-anniversary. Accessed 8 Aug 2017.

Thornton, Steve. "1199 History-PowerPoint Presentation." 2008.

Thornton, Steve. "Introduction: Welcome. This is the Shoeleather History Charter Oak Walking Tour." Handout during Shoeleather Walking Tour, 11 Jul 2017.

Cambar Edwards
Kimberly Hall North, Windsor

Women's Right to Fight: The Story Behind My Story

The year was 1900, when ladies had no legal right to vote and had no right to stand and speak in public gatherings. Hundreds of women, out of self-determination and love for their families, went out of the boundaries of their yard, house, and families' farm land to work where they can exchange their precious time for money. They were like young navigators experimenting with work outside of their homes and farm land. The working conditions were unacceptable compared to today's modern facilities. The workplace then was only conducive for men. Women were looked down upon, and they had no form of equality in society. Women had to work hard within their households and twice as hard in a public setting. They had to be very brave to step out of the kitchen and off of the farm to go into a factory to work. Despite all of the criticism, they held their heads up and put their minds and bodies to getting the work done. Although working outside the home was considered at the time a man's job, the women still worked their fingers and skin to the bone.

Going on the Shoelcather Walking Tour given by historian and activist, Steve Thornton, enlightened me to ordinary people who did not get their due recognition in history. All various sites and people were intriguing and important stories, but the story of the Capewell Horse Nail Factory drew my attention.

Steve Thornton began telling the tour members about the history of the Capewell Horse Nail Factory. In 1902, the Capewell Factory already had two unions. There was a machinist union for the men and a sorters and packers union for women. Thornton continued with the story. The factory burned down in 1902 and put everyone out of work. George Capewell ordered the women back to work to sort through rubble for good nails, and he explained to them that they would be getting less pay than their regular pay rate because it was "not their real job" (Thornton). The women complained that the job was harder. Not only was the job harder, but it was dirty and way more dangerous than their regular jobs. They could have seriously pricked their fingers while gathering up the nails. Finally, on August 19, 1902, the woman mobilized their union to go out on strike. Despite the low unionism, with help from families and union organizers they kept the fight going on about four months. Thornton explained how Samuel Gompers, then president of the American Federation of Labor, stepped in to help resolve the strike. The women went back to work in December of 1902.

This strike must have been one of the hardest fights the women had to endure. The women had no support coming from their male coworkers who worked with the machines. It was good to learn that the ladies stood up for their rights and fair pay and took the risk of going on strike. I believe that this strike made women more determined and resilient to stand up together for rights of all women. They led a cause, and they were noticed. They broke new ground for women.

Thornton explained about a second strike at the Capewell factory. "On April 10, 1935 with a shrinking demand for their product Capewell laid off 8 men, citing lack of work" (Thornton). What a coincidence, most of the workers who got laid off were union leaders. The struggle and the fight intensified, and the unionized men decided not do their jobs, but they still showed up to work and "they stayed by their machines and refused to move" (Thornton). This was considered to be a 'sit-down' strike. The famous 1936-37 Ford Motor Company strike in Flint Michigan followed suit a year and half after the great move of the Capewell unionized men. Thornton mentioned that the newspapers described it as a "folded arms strike", and a "Gandhi strike". This severe tactic of striking took off like a wild fire across the country. It was very successful in many situations, but this very brave tactic was eventually banned by the courts and "discouraged by the national union heads" (Thornton). The men agreed to share the lay-off hours in order to come back to work, so all men could come back to work.

The lesson learned from the strong solidarity of the workers of Capewell is that strength comes in numbers, persistence, and patience. The factory workers then are the same as we are today. Their struggles are not much different from our struggles today. Unity drives growth and much needed social change.

My Story

I have been working in the health care industry for 21 years, and I have been a delegate of the District 1199, SEIU since 2004. I have seen the struggles and determination of the Union members to fight for better wages, better working conditions, better health benefits and pensions, and better education for all workers. So, the Capewell story of its men's and women's unions and strikes were compelling and made me want to work more diligently to better support my Chapter of the 1199 Union. The significance of the Capewell strikes, both men's and women's, voices the theme of unity, solidarity, and that there is strength in numbers. I feel that these men and women had a tremendous amount of courage and patience to endure the struggles and not give up. As someone from the 1199 Union stated, "an attack on one worker is an attack on all workers". No matter what your gender, the injustices on one person, goes for all. Union members must unite and stand together to achieve their goal of human rights and dignity in the workplace.

Before becoming a Union delegate, as a non-union worker in 2003, there was such a hardship on the workers in my Chapter. We were overworked and

62

under paid, and it was during that time that I began to hear about the 1199 Union. I then asked what can it do for myself and the workers. I heard about the great work Jerry Brown, Carmen Boudier, and Rose Brown had been doing for workers. It was quoted to me that "Carmen is a Jamaican". I told myself if she can do it, I can do it. So, I began talking with my coworkers about standing up together for better pay and working conditions and treatment on the job. I and other Union Leaders mobilized the workers to bring in the Union to Kimberly Hall North. Trying to bring in the Union was the fight of my life. Finally, we had an election deciding the outcome of having the Union represent us at Kimberly Hall North. Although I worried whether I would have a job the day after the election, I still kept communications open with coworkers. The outcome was that we won the right to be represented by SEIU-1199.

Geogette Gagnon was a past worker at Capewell and a worker for Avery Heights Nursing Home facility. She was an outstanding Certified Nurses Aide and a diligent delegate at her Chapter under the leadership of Jerry Brown and Carmen Boudier. I learned from them that it is important to know what the Union members' and co-workers' issues are and how to go about to make changes. I learned that sticking together makes a strong team. Most of the time, their issues are my issues. They were my mentors who helped me become a Union delegate.

I have helped to lead my Kimberly Hall North Chapter of my 1199 Union in a lot of accomplishments over the years. One of the first accomplishments was when the management wanted to reduce the pay rate of two senior workers who were locked into a special rate agreement over a ten-year period. Through the action of the Union, the two senior workers won the right to keep their special pay rate. Another time, the Director of Nursing extended an offer for lunch for the Delegates only so she could get to know them. I told her that she would need to open lunch to all Union members who were working that day. I insisted that the lunch must be for all Union members, but she refused, so I told her we will not meet as it looked like she was trying to buy out the Delegates. Next, the same Nursing Director wanted to stop CNAs from going out about 15 minutes before the end of the shift to start cleaning and digging out their cars after snow storms, but the Union intervened again, and we won again. Importantly, by standing together we had the power to win. Somewhat later in time, the Union members strategically reported on the company's survey that we needed electric beds instead of the crank-type beds and we won again. This accomplishment was so big; it had all members and patients and family smiling and happy that they all got a new bed.

A very important accomplishment occurred when the Union negotiated our contract in 2005. We got a pay increase, kept our health insurance, and won the ability to join the 1199 Training &Upgrading Fund for education purposes. This was a big win for all!

Years later, during late 2014, about 27 nursing homes were going to go out on strike for pay increase, better health insurance, and a pension that we did not have. In the 2015 negotiations, we rallied for our 'Stand Up for 15' ($15 per hour minimum pay rate) and our pension. We won our pension, and we were somewhat successful in obtaining close to the $15.00 per hour. This shows that if we stand together, we can achieve our goals. The fight may be long and difficult, but, the fights will resume on another day, with another boss, and with another department. Understanding this, I must stay focused knowing that what I am doing today is to better the workplace for the future.

To conclude, I have identified my struggle with the Capewell Horse Nail Factory women because they had endured and mastered the injustices against them and their Union. Their struggles were very similar to what I have gone through and am going through as a leader and delegate for SEIU District 1199. We learn from each other, we learn from our mistakes, and each day is renewed with love and the mindset for our family, work family, Union members, our extended family, community, and church family. We all need each other to survive. It is so delightful and encouraging knowing that I am standing with a strong organization that is standing up against social injustices and promoting human dignity. It is important to take the time to learn the full potential of our incredible Union and take full advantage of what it offers. The Union is a career builder, a strong motivator, politically savvy, and supports all its members and the community, too. The Union pledges to fight for each and every one, and fighting for one is a fight for all!

Works Cited

Thornton, Steve. "Introduction: Welcome. This is the Shoeleather History Charter Oak walking tour." 11 Jul 17.

What have I done since 2003—accomplishments, winning, how people feel about unity and the Union.

Carol Harrison
Touchpoints at Bloomfield

The Unknown

I ventured out one summer evening with my class-mates of the creative writing class on The Shoeleather Walking Tour led by historian Steve Thornton to learn about places and people of the past around the Charter Oak Avenue area of Hartford. I was very intrigued by the history of Hartford. I have been living only twenty minutes outside of Hartford for the past 27 years, and I never knew much about its history. That July day, I learned many things; however, there was one story that stood out to me. The most inter-esting story was about Father Jerzy Popieluszko.

Jerzy Popieluszko was a priest in the Catholic Church in Poland in the early 1980's. He believed in solidarity and freedom. Steve Thornton gave us a quote from Father Popieluszko that reads, "Truth never changes. It cannot be destroyed by any deci-sion or legal act, telling the truth with courage is a way leading directly to freedom. A man who tells the truth is a free man despite external slavery, impris-onment or custody." This is a powerful statement because the truth means that it's something that you believe in, and it cannot be changed or altered. For instance, what is in the Bible is true about religion and humanity and living an honorable life.

Father Popieluszko stood for the truth, equal rights, and solidarity to fight for the Polish people's right to freedom and freedom of their voices. He stood for the people who had no say. He was their voice of truth, and his lectures "were broadcast by Radio Free Europe" to the people of Poland ("The Making of a Martyr"). In 1980, he connected with the steel-workers union strike as their chaplain (Thornton). He became famous throughout Poland and around the world for his service to humanity; however, the Communist government politicians and officials hated that his voice was so strongly influencing the people. They tried to kill him; however, he escaped, but finally, the Communists succeeded in killing him for his beliefs.

There is a saying that goes something like, "You have to stand for what you believe in, or you'll stand for nothing". As Steve Thornton said, Father Popieluszko was "a public voice from the pulpit," and he spoke the truth about what he believed in, and he died for what he believed in. Importantly, Father Popieluszko carried the truth with him in death.

As for me, Father Popieluszko was important because he opened doors for the people of Poland through the work he did. He helped take down the barriers to freedom, and for me, I am lucky that in the United States, I can speak openly about what is on my mind. Regarding my Union, he paved the way for workers to stand together and unify to make their voices heard. His words have empowered me and others to stand together for what we believe in and in every circumstance of our lives. I feel his work towards freedom has helped pave the way for his generation, my generation, and for future generations to come.

I have been a member of the 1199 Union for 25 years now, and I have seen the struggles from the first year until now. And, I saw how hard we have worked night and day to establish what we truly believe in. The Union members fought for better opportunities, better benefits, job security, and continuing education, and it was worth it. We have won many of our fights because we stood together, which is what Father Jerzy Popieluszko believed in--the strength of Solidarity. Jerzy Popieluszko gave his life for what he believed in, and today, we can find strength in his words, and we will continue to fight for our rights for generations to come.

For future members of the 1199 Union and many other unions, I would like to advise these members to stick together and fight for what they believe in and to remember to stand up for what you believe and make your voices heard.

Works Cited

"The Making of a Martyr – The Murder of Father Jerzy Popieluszko." Association of Diplomatic Studies and Training, 2015, adst.org/2105/10/the-making-of-a-martyr-the-murder-of-father-jerzy-popieluszko/. Accessed 1 Aug 2017.

Thornton, Steve. "Introduction: Welcome. This is the Shoeleather History Charter Oak walking tour." Handout during Shoeleather Walking Tour, Steve Thornton, 11 Jul 2017.

Thornton, Steve. "Shoeleather Walking Tour." Quote Handout during Shoeleather Walking Tour, Steve Thornton, 11 Jul 2017.

Donna Monteith
Touchpoints at Farmington

Father Jerzy Popieluszko Gave Me Strength

The 1199 Training and Upgrading Fund offered a creative writing class, and I was happy to join. I had taken another class with Alma Farnsworth last summer. She is a wonderful teacher. Our summer 2017 class took a tour around the Charter Oak section of Hartford having Steve Thornton, historian, as our tour guide. It was a wonderful experience. Several people and places stood out for me. The stories of the Charter Oak, Richard Gatling, Capewell Horse Nail Factory, Colt Firearms Factory, Tom Standish, Carmen Boudier, and Father Jerzy Popieluszko were very interesting. I have lived in Hartford for over thirty years, and I run up and down these streets every day and have never taken the time to look at some of these street names nor knew of their history. I will never forget the stories told by Steve Thornton.

After learning what Steve Thornton taught about Father Jerzy Popieluszko, I decided to do more research on Father Popuieluszko. He was a man of great interest to me. To get to the Union office, I have to drive down Popieluszko Street, and I did not know the history about it. Now, every Polish person I meet, I ask "Did you ever hear of Father Popieluszko?". Most would reply yes, and I would go on to ask more questions or fill them in with what I have learned.

Father Popieluszko was a political activist for the social movements and rights of the Polish people. He was a martyr who fought against communism, and he led a campaign for change, freedom, and rights. Born on September 14, 1947, Father Popieluszko lived in Poland and was ordained as a minister in 1972 after serving two years in the Polish army ("Blessed Jerzy"). His sermons took a firm stance against communism and incited many to protest. The church was the only place where people were able to speak whatever they wanted publicly without being chastised or being arrested. Due to poor health in 1979, he became a chaplain to medical workers, and in August 1980, "he celebrated Mass for striking [Steel] workers" ("Blessed Jerzy").

In August 1980, the Trade Union known as "Solidarity formed in Poland and was independent of the Polish government" (Thornton). Father Popieluszko continued to speak out against political injustice; however, in October 1984, he was beaten and thrown into a river to die. He was killed for speaking out for people's rights and telling the truth; he was accused "of excessive use of his rights as a priest on effort to cause harm to the People's Republic of Poland" ("Blessed Jerzy").

Being a member of the 1199 Union, I can associate with Father Popieluszko and his struggles for Solidarity. I have great respect for Father Popieluszko. He was a man of great courage. Virgo's are known to be great leaders. I have worked in the healthcare field for over twenty five years, and about two years ago, I

was selected to be an 1199 Union delegate. I did no
want to be one, but my co-workers chose me because
I have a strong voice.

Father Popieluszko paved the way for us, so it's
only right that we pay him homage for all the work
he had done. Being a Union member, I know many
people who are afraid to speak out against injustice
and discrimination and speak for human rights and
fair treatment in the workplace for fear of being repri-
manded. But, as for me, I will not stand for injustices,
not even racism. I will not stand for bullying. I will
not see my co-workers being taken advantage of and
having to keep a closed mouth. Many times people
are scared to speak out in fear of losing their jobs.
We all need our jobs, but we have to stand up for
our rights. I look to Father Popieluszko to have his
strength and courage to speak up as needed and help
lead my co-workers.

The Union has been very helpful in getting our
voices heard, helping us get back into school, and
making sure we have healthcare coverage, time off,
decent salaries, retirement, and job security. The
Union fights for our rights, and it is an advocate for
staffing and opportunities.

At times working in this industry, I feel like
throwing in the towel, but Father Popieluszko never
did, and I will not either. Management would have
to fire me because I am only fighting for my rights. If
only other co-workers could be as brave, so I am there
to support them. These last few months have been
hectic, so I called the Union to come to my health-

...are facility to understand what was going on in the workplace. All of management had been scrambling around trying to make sure everything seemed to be running perfectly, now that I had called the Union. It had been years since we had a staff meeting, and just last week management had a meeting about 'Safety in the Workplace'. Never mind safety, how about saving our backs. Management was keeping us short staffed every single day, while they were still getting a paycheck or sometime big bonuses. The Union is there to make sure we employees get treated fairly. Union members need to come together to make our workplace better. Through the Union, our voices can be heard.

Last year when we were in negotiations about our bargaining agreement, I conducted a survey at my job to see who was willing to go on a strike if we had to do so. Most of the workers did not want to strike, which left me in tears. I was not seeing unity in my fellow co-workers. If there is no unity, we do not stand a chance to move ahead. Father Popieluszko died for a cause, so I knew I had to stand up for what I thought was right. Some people have not taken the time out to find out what the Union is about, but they want to reap all the benefits. I was so disappointed with my co-workers when we had a collective bargaining with the bosses. There were only two of us who showed up from our facility. If it was not for other homes attending, we would look stupid. My co-workers all wanted to know what happened at the meeting the next day. I had to tell them that the Union could be a stronger voice if they show up. Luckily, with all the other staff members from other facilities at the bargaining meeting, we showed our power and strength in our numbers. We ended up getting our raise and more benefits. I am so glad that I had the strength to stand up for all of our rights.

A Union is an organization for every member of the Union, using its collective strength to prevent management from doing whatever they want with their employees. The Union helps members to attain healthcare coverage, time off, decent salaries, retirements, job security, no cost education, and it advocates for better staffing and opportunities. If it was not for being unionized, management could fire without justifiable cause. Members of the 1199 Union have been able to achieve high job standards in America for healthcare workers. Father Popieluszko led his people to fight or strike for their civil rights, and the only way workers will win better pay, benefits, and respect is by having the courage to stand up for one another, their patients, and their families.

Works Cited

Szczygiel, Veronica. "Blessed Jerzy Popieluszko, Priest, Martyr." *St. Stanislaus Kostka*, 2011, Ststanskostka.org. Accessed 1 Aug 2017.

Thornton, Steve. "Introduction: Welcome. This is the Shoeleather History Charter Oak walking tour." *Handout during Shoeleather Walking Tour*, Steve Thornton, 11 Jul 2017.

BOOK THREE

STORIES FROM THE 1199NE TRAINING FUND CONFERENCE

Steve Bender

Introduction

I love these stories. Caregivers are remarkable people, whether they give care in a nursing home or in someone's home. Everyone can't do this work, but thank goodness there are people like the writers in this book who work day after day, giving beautiful, compassionate care to those who need it most.

Their work is hidden to much of the world, but their stories deserve to be told. Reading these stories puts a smile on my face. Thanks to all the writers who took the time to tell their stories. Many of the writers chose to tell about their lives as caregivers. Others chose to write about other sides to themselves, to give us insight into their lives. These stories are important, and they have lessons for us all.

Steve Bender
Executive Director
1199 Training Fund
Hartford, Connecticut

Marian Barracks
Amberwoods of Farmington (Retired)

I Think I Am One of the Miracles

It was the year 2014 when I was pulled over by the police going to work. It was a snowy day. I had to get to work by 8 AM, so I was driving very fast, or that is what they thought. In reality I was driving only 40 miles per hour. By this time someone called the police because I was driving too slow. It happened that there was a sign posted, "Drive With Caution," and so I told the police. He told me, "Thank you for thinking of safety."

So I went to work, when I find out I was walking as if I was drunk, even though I don't drink. That was when I knew I had to go to the doctor. I made an appointment to see the doctor. The relation between me and my doctor is very good, so he told me to come right away, which I did. I told him my symptoms, and he sent me to the hospital, where they did an MRI of the brain, and they saw a mass there.

I was told they have never seen anything like what they saw. For the next two weeks I was in the hospital in Hartford. Then I was moved to Yale, in New Haven. That was where I was told what was wrong: I probably have what's known as swelling of the brainstem. The doctors call it "CLIPPER," but it's not the electric kind.

The doctor I am seeing sent me to one of the world's best neurologists in New York City. I arrived two hours late, but he waited for me. After seeing this doctor, we spoke for a while, after which he said to me, "I will never get better."

That was not the news I was looking for. Nevertheless, I shook his hand and said, "Thank you, my God will see me through."

He turned to me and said, "Good luck," and with that saying, I left.

I went back to see my doctor, and he started me on a lot of meds and instructions, which I follow. I belong to a praying church, and I am also a praying person. If one could see me back then, and could see me now, I think I am one of the miracles.

NEW ENGLAND HEALTH CARE EMPLOYEES UNION

DISTRICT 1199

AND THE CONNECTICUT NURSING HOMES

T&U

TRAINING & UPGRADING

FUND

Sandy Bellino
Personal Care Attendant

Brave In Graves

Hello, my name is Sandy. Welcome to "A Mile in our 84's." Born my mother's only daughter into a B.I.G. family. Big as in "Big In Giving." Brave In Graves.

I was raised in the 80's by my European maternal grandmother Big Marie. Big Marie was a legally blind live-in caregiver and humanitarian who lost her eyesight, but never her vision, for which I am truly blessed. Fortunately, my great aunt Muff and my great aunt Mitz, who was an LPN, was an 1199 member since the 70's. My great uncle Ed and grandfather Billy I would later find out in my late teens were the foundation of morals and family support. From my early upbringing, Uncle Ed and Grandfather Bill guided me into the strong work ethic and family values that raised me up and over to the woman I am becoming today.

I know you're wondering what does it mean, "B.I.G?" Well, we're all "big" in our own way. Ah, mine is Graves disease, which is only a title, not a definition or diagnosis I let claim me. Graves is a hyperthyroid auto-immune disease I was diagnosed with in my late 20's.

Imagine leading an outgoing, athletic lifestyle full of energy and ambition, then one day having a doctor say, "We want to run some tests on your thyroid gland and take some blood work to screen you for thyroid cancer."

"WHAT?!" I yelped in shock, "there must be a mix-up, I don't feel sick or have a family history, so this has to be a mistake," said I, the fearless caregiver to the bearer of bad news.

No need to get worried, I was told, Graves Disease isn't common in women of color in my age, they just needed to run a series of tests over the next 48 hours and observe me overnight.

I didn't know what being strong or the real definition of "fight like a girl" was, until my battle with Graves taught me that my purpose is to survive, because I was born to stand out. I am a B.I.G. girl in small packaging!!

To be continued.

Thank you,
Sandy

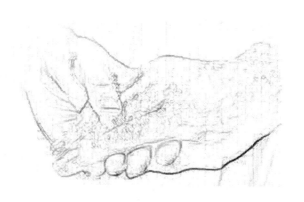

Delroy Bennett
Saint Mary Home, West Hartford

Why I Do What I Do

Why do I do what I do, with so much more that I could do? But it is worth every moment of my time.

You may ask the question, "What is there for me to do, apart from being a care giver?" I am from Jamaica. Starting as a young man at the age of 18, I went to work at a bakery. The boss promised to pay me $8.00 per day. When pay day came, he paid me $7.00.

I took the seven dollars, and that was the first day and the last day I worked for him. But I did take note of the way he built his oven. So I went back to the country. I got a round metal drum-pan and cut a door in it. I was on my way to making an oven.

My father asked me, "Son, what are you doing?"

I said to him, "You will see."

I placed the metal container in the ground. And I remember I baked for the first time two pounds of flour. The next door neighbor came over and he bought two of my cakes. From that day my life was changed: I was a baker. I make three Jamaican cakes: bulla, rock cake and cut cake.

That was 33 years ago. I am here in America and still doing it. In between, I go to trade school to learn cabinet making, and I still do that now and then.

The question came about: Why do I do what I am doing, working as a CNA? I love when I walk in to my work and it is 3 pm. I say "Good morning," and someone will say "Good morning" back to me. Some will tell me, "It's not morning, it's afternoon!" and we start a conversation. One would be sitting at the desk and would be announcing the time. He would say, "It is 3:25," and I would say, "You are sure about that?" And he would say, "Pretty sure," and I would say, "It is 3:24 and ½."

These are some of the reasons I love my job, and I love people. We never know what and where we will stop next. I remember taking care of the son, then the father. I don't lose hope. We never know. Just like a baker: you take your chance — some cakes will burn, some will come out just right.

Take a chance, and enjoy what you make.

Jayne E.S. Gary
60 West, Rocky Hill

A Gentleman in the Facility

My story is about a gentleman in the facility where I work.

This man came into the facility. He was some-what grateful. He had been at the facility for abut 1 ½ years, give or take. Shortly after arriving at the facility he began to exhibit certain behaviors: falling on the floor on purpose; happy one moment, unhappy the next; shouting out that he is so unhappy here at the facility; and how he wanted to return to where he had come from, CVH. He said he needed to make some money, like he did at CVH.

Now that he has been at our facility for over a year, these behaviors and speeches are less frequent, but they remain all the same. His desire to leave the facility and such puzzles me sometimes, and it saddens me.

He has expressed to me how he would rather "live under a bridge in a box than live at this place." He has shouted at me. I find it very interesting that he requires assistance to perform some daily activities: washing, dressing, sometimes eating (holding his utensils), lifting his feet onto the bed or pulling the blanket/comforter up over himself. Yet, he would purposefully want to escape, and he has tried to leave the facility. He knows he needs help, and he will ask for assistance for his getaway.

Although he is not an elderly man, life has taken a toll on his body. He still has the presence of a fancy man. He is tall, nice looking well built and cares about his appearance. Also, he used to express his desire to return to CVH. However, now he expresses a desire to go someplace far away.

He no longer expresses a desire of attaining an apartment or a desire for even a room in a rooming house, or for a job. He does not talk about where he will get food or feed himself.

I'm interested in what he actually needs or wants at this time in his life. Sometimes we can't make everyone happy or content, but we keep trying.

Lucille Green
Saint Mary Home, West Hartford

I Do Care

Oftentimes people always have this mentality that their job needs them and they can always quit. No one should ever feel that way. No job needs them, because you can be replaced in seconds, and you are history. I always tell myself that no job needs me, I need the job. So I will have to do my best and follow directions and respect rules and regulations.

There are these words that I avoid using, "I don't care." I will always try to replace them with, "I do care."

There was a little boy, whenever his mother tries to sway him away from things that are dangerous, he would tell her, "I don't care." One day he was playing outside and there was an alligator on his lawn. She tried to tell him to stay inside, because the alligator will attack him. He said to her, "I don't care." The alligator grabbed his leg. He started, "Mom! Mom! I DO care!"

The ambulance came and took him to the hospital. His mom was very worried that he was going to lose his leg. She prayed very hard that he would not lose his leg. The greatest moment of their lives was after the doctor came out and said, "Mom, we saved his leg."

She had faith that her prayers would be answered. She thanked God for answering her prayer.

This was a lesson well learnt. He apologized, "Mom, I will never use the words 'I don't care' again. Mom, you were so right, and I will always adhere to your instructions. I do care."

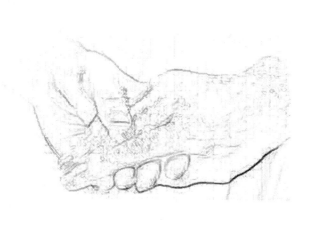

Kenroy Hinds
Saint Mary Home, West Hartford

My Best Friend

My mother was my best friend, my counselor, and my adviser. At the age of eleven years old, I was not doing well in school. She brought me up to military camp, which is an army base in Jamaica, so I could join the Cadet Force Band. I played the tuba.

Attending military camp and joining the band was the best move of my life. I started to do well in school. My band won the festival competition in 1984 in Jamaica. It was a proud day for me, and for my mom.

Then I got a scholarship to attend the Jamaican School of Music. When I was at the Jamaican School I got to play with the Jamaican Philharmonic Orchestra, and the National Choral of Jamaica. We played all over Jamaica, and even on other islands in the Caribbean.

In 1986 I became the Head Boy at my high school because of my mother pushing me to join the Cadet Force Band. It helped me a lot.

My mother is resting now at the Garden of Peace in Atlanta, Georgia. I miss her words of advice to me up to today, and I carry those words with me wherever I go: Learn to play the tuba; become a business man; hold onto your dreams.

When our band played at the Jamaican Festival, we played Stevie Wonder's *Ribbon in the Sky*. When the lovely heavenly choir in Heaven sings, I like to think that my mom always listens for the tuba.

Marvalene Hinds
Personal Care Attendant

Thankful and Not Sad

This is my life story after I left Jamaica. I was twenty-one years old when I came to the United States from Jamaica. It was a very sad and lonely time for me. I knew just a few people. I was sad most of the time. I would write my mother telling her I wanted to return home to Jamaica, but she said to stay.

But after a couple of months I got a job at a restaurant. One year after, I went to Capital Community College, where I earned my CNA certificate. My life started to change for the better. No more sad feelings. I got married, had two children, and found a job in a nursing home, where I worked for 18 years.

After ten years I earned my high school diploma from the Training and Upgrading Fund. I am very thankful for the 1199 Training Fund and for the teachers who helped me to achieve my high school diploma.

Clarissa Johnson
Personal Care Attendant

Each One, Teach One

Greetings. Clarissa Johnson is my name: yes, this one fabulous word that identifies you at birth and is with us until we leave this world. We surround ourselves with people we love and care for.

I've given care to someone in need for years, from the age of twelve. Three dollars, twenty-five cents was my pay for a community-based homecare company.

One of God's commandments is that you "love" one another as God has loved each and every one of us. A few years back, after 27 years working at a nursing home that closed, I had the opportunity to work through a program at a school grade pre-K to eighth grade, in the nursing department. I can always hear the school nurse, an RN, say to the students, "Each one, teach one."

Those words she said were so true and powerful. When you look into someone's eyes, when you care for that elderly, sick, disabled or even depressed person, there's a story behind their lives. You just can't help but have love and feel compassion for a family member, friend or your clients.

Yes, we may think exercising, healthy eating, reading hundreds of books will make us superhuman, defiant, and invincible.

Being a caregiver at the age of twelve and a half prepared me for the health field. I loved to hear stories of their children, extended family and friends, and what they accomplished in life until they couldn't remember where they were and couldn't recognize faces or dress themselves.

As a caregiver, your consumer (client) looks forward to seeing you coming, knowing some of their extended family has moved, sometimes even to another country, and now they are an only child again.

Each day I got up and went to that three hour job after school, which prepared me as a companion, home health care worker, CNA, PCA. I bring joy to someone's life.

After my training as a CNA, I had an assignment, and there was a patient of mine who survived the holocaust. With your assignment, you have footnotes of the patient's criteria and daily activities, called a care plan. In red the assignment said, "No shower, give patient bed bath." The nurse explained that the client was a survivor of the holocaust who couldn't be exposed to the silver of the shower room, because of her memories of the past.

Her walker was covered with blue duct tape so she would not be reminded of the silver-colored metal in the death camp. Each day I would care for her and sit and talk to her. We would walk by the shower room and look in as I stood beside her. Also, she would see other CNA's bringing clients into the shower.

The walker that she used to walk with had blue

duct tape covering every inch, I wondered why. She had fear of the walls and the silver bars in the shower room. She was also fearful of her walker's shiny metal, which reminded her of the death camp.

The great words that someone said, "The only thing you have to fear is fear itself" rang true. That day fear left that patient's life. It took time to get her to take a shower. Her mind was reflecting back to a horrific part in her life. With a caring heart and compassion, and most of all love, she overcame her fear and attended many recreation activities with other residents.

Delores Keith
Touchpoints at Bloomfield

The Roan Women In My Life

I'll start with growing up, not with one mom, I had three other moms. As I grew up and started my family, my mom and my aunts played a big role in my adult life. Whenever I needed food or clothing for my family, my aunts were always there for me. No matter what I asked for, they made sure I had what I needed.

Intros to the Roan women: Elizabeth Smith, Margaret Thomas, Priscella Howard and Janet Harris. My mom, Elizabeth R. Smith, was the oldest daughter of a family of four girls and six boys. My mom was the oldest of the sisters. Then there was Aunt Margaret, then Aunt Priscella, then the youngest, my Aunt Janet. Each woman was strong in their own right, caring and giving advice was their thing. Always ready to give, and always ready to tell a story.

When I had my first daughter 25 years ago, I started doing their hair every two weeks. We'd go to Aunt Priscella's house and eat lunch and do hair. We'd laugh and talk about everything.

Now, as we ate lunch before doing hair, we'd talk about old times. Aunt Priscella and mom always argued about who helped my gran the most. Aunt Margaret was always quiet. She never debated with Aunt Priscella, but would talk about her when she got home. Now Aunt Janet never got her hair done because she thought her hair was perfect, and I was okay with that. But when I needed food, I could go to her house and go in the basement and come out with at least four bags of groceries. Aunt Janet was the bomb.

This was my time to learn about my family history. I loved these times, and so my family grew. I'd bring my kids with me to sit in my aunt's living room until I was done doing the hair.

Now I'm just touching certain points in this story, otherwise I'd be writing all day. As years progressed, so did all our ages, including mine, but I still did their hair and enjoyed doing so.

My Aunt Janet was the first to pass away. She had cancer. Her first year, she kept to herself. Her second, she told her family, and we all were there for her until her last day on earth.

Aunt Priscella was next. She fell and hit her head, cracked her skull and was gone within a month of that happening.

Now my mom and Aunt Margaret held on until their 90's, plus. These two were always close sisters. A year and a half apart in age, they married brothers and were friends as well as sisters. Aunt Margaret went to a nursing home first. She kept falling at home, so my cousin Cheryl made the decision for her mom. My mom went a year after Aunt Margaret went. It was an experience for all of us.

Aunt Margaret had dementia, and it progressed before my mom. So mom couldn't understand why her sister slept all the time, even though when I was a teenager, that's all my mom and dad did was sleep.

We never went anywhere because they were always tired. But that's another chapter of my life.

Now, mom was only in the nursing home a year and a half, whereas Aunt Margaret was about two years. Mom passed on November 34, 2012, and Aunt Margaret died five months after that. We figured her sisters called her home with them.

Okay, so now I'm here, no one to talk to, no one to tell me a story. No hair to be done. I was lost. I couldn't connect with my cousins, because my connection was my aunts. I felt like a lost puppy, until one day two years ago, I went back to school and got my CNA certificate, and now I'm in a facility with older people, and I know in my heart that this is where I belong.

So now I do hair, listen to stories, and share *my* stories. I hug my clients and feel like I have purpose again. My mom and aunts would be proud of me.

Esmine Martin
Greensprings Healthcare and Rehabilitation,
East Hartford

Unprofessional Coworkers

In today's world there are many coworkers who behave professionally, and there are those who act unprofessionally in their work environment. I have worked in a nursing home for many years. Many people who work with me know that I do my work very professionally. I respect my nurses and all my coworkers, and my residents as well.

Sometimes I work on the evening shift. On every other weekend I work the seven-to-three shift. Sometimes people call out on the evening shift.

Many time the supervisor asks me to stay over for the evening shift, and I always refuse. It so happened that the first time I planned to work a double shift, on that day it was Saturday, a coworker was fighting for the assignment that I planned to do. The regular evening shift aide was off that weekend.

Another aide wanted to do that assignment, but because of the argument, she decided to go home. Usually there would be four of us aides working on my ward. But on that evening we ended up working short, with only three staff members on duty. This was a very tiring evening for me. I had extra work to do on the double shift, when I was already tired staying over.

This particular aide acted in an unprofessional manner. She was yelling at the nurse and raising her voice in the presence of the residents. I was very calm and soft spoken. I went to work on the opposite side of the floor, so she, the angry one, ended up working by herself.

I was upset over the whole situation of how the staff member was working The matter was reported to the supervisor, and I was glad to be an example of a professional care giver putting my residents first.

Sunitta McCarthy
Harrington Court, Colchester

My Open Heart

While I was waiting for my immigration documents, at that time I couldn't drive, and only stayed home. One day I got brochures from an adult education program. I decided to go to school and start ESL classes. I saw they had room at a GED class. I decided to take the GED class, and I passed the test. After passing all my exams, the manager who worked at a nursing home talked to me and asked, "Would you like to clean people's butts?"

At that time I did not really understand what it means. I said, "Sure." I took another class at the community college and got a job as a CNA every evening. I still continue with education, and I am moving to the highest level. Education for me is like food: it helps to keep me alive. Now I am attending the Radiology Program and hope to graduate in 2019.

I like the CNA job because I feel connected to my mom and my dad. I worked in a different town from my mom. When I went home to see my mom, she always talked to me about what she wanted. I listened and did what she needed.

One night I was very busy taking care of patients. I had a new patient, who had moved in to our facility three nights before. I saw a picture of her and her husband. I asked her, "Who's that handsome man?"

After that I had a chance to hear her story and

learn how she felt. She cried and hugged me. "I am very lonely and scared to stay here."

I realized that the one minute that I stopped to listen to her made her feel warm: she was having me as a friend. Later she was enjoying her final home and not feeling lonely!

I always smile when I think about that night. Going to work, I feel I am going to see my family.

NEW ENGLAND HEALTH CARE EMPLOYEES UNION

DISTRICT 1199

AND THE CONNECTICUT NURSING HOMES

T&U

TRAINING & UPGRADING

FUND

Paulet McDonald
Greensprings Health Center, East Hartford

Good-bye, Mr. Brown

In 1996 I had the ambition of becoming a nurse, so I attended Channer School of Nursing in Montego Bay, Jamaica. I was a student nurse and a caregiver (a CNA) in the hospital.

I was assigned to several patients, but there was one who touched my heart. His name was Mr. William Brown.

Mr. Brown and I became connected because he was from my district and knew me when I was a small child. He told me stories about me at a tender age of eight years old.

His fondest memory of me was bringing me my milk in the morning. Also taking me to see my godmother. He told a lot of stories about me for his students and they laughed. Sometimes they laughed so hard.

On July 3, 1997, I went to school. I ran upstairs to say hi to Mr. Brown and to pick up my assignment for the day. Miss Hines said, "I will put you in charge of Mr. Brown today, he has been asking for you all night."

So I said, "Okay." I then went over to see him. I said my good morning, but he wasn't looking very well. I told him I will be back. I went to the charge nurse and told her to please call Dr. Channer, and then I left for class.

Upon returning I went to change him and fed him breakfast, for he had soiled his bed. Mr. Brown looked me in the eye and said, "Thank you, I love you. I am sorry I left that for you."

I told him, "It's okay, that's my job, and I love you." I added, "Thank you for all you did for me when I was younger."

I left the room for but a short while. I went back to give him care, and right in the midst he squeezed my hand and closed his eyes.

And that was goodbye from my dear Mr. Brown.

.

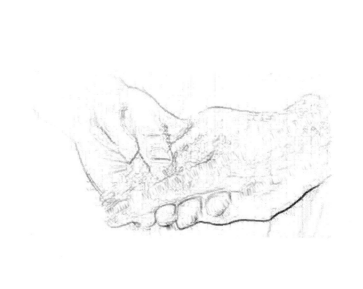

Kathleeen Mendola
Personal Care Attendant

Trying To Make a Better Living

For the past 23 years, I have worked as a CNA and PCA. I worked in a Connecticut nursing home for nineteen years, For the past four years I have worked in home care. My experience in the medical field has become a success. I have become a part of 1199 and grown in the field. I am currently in school for my two year degree in political science. Since I have been involved with 1199, politics has become a big interest in what I'd like to do as a career.

As of now I am currently employed at AFLAC as a benefits consultant and have grown more. I enjoy meeting new people from day to day. I'm still working part-time as a PCA to be a part of my union, 1199.

For the past four years, I feel my union has made me grow and I feel more confident in my career as I continue working with AFLAC, though, with AFLAC I find it more difficult to make a living because my pay is based on commission.

I will say that my main goal is to get my two year degree in political science. I feel that I will grow more in the field, something that I would enjoy more. I also have earned leadership in 1199, which has helped me grow more and more to take on more roles.

As I work as a benefits consultant at AFLAC, I find being my own boss is a little easier. I can make my own hours day to day, meeting district managers and clients. I also find we are on the same page. Working together is a lot easier, though when I find it difficult to work out a contract, my district manager pulls in and helps me.

My career has taken off in a lot of good ways.

Donna Monteith
Touchpoints at Farmington

Washington, Here I Come

Wow. This is about the sixth time I am writing a story. My first story was with Steve Bender; he asked me to join a writing class. I was apprehensive at first, then he convinced me I can do it.

I wrote a poem about Mr. Johnson. Then I turned it into a story. Steve was so impressed that he invited the HeartBeat Ensemble to take a look at it. They loved it and decided to create a play out of my story. The theater company first performed my play at a church, then at the C.N.A. conference. It was also performed in downtown Hartford. I was so pleased, I joined every class thereafter.

Tim Sheard offered a writing class which I also attended. When he asked me what was I going to write about, I wrote about "Me and My Big Mouth." My story was published in a book, *With Our Loving Hands*, along with other union members.

Steve called me up and said they were looking for some students to write an essay to the Big Shots in Washington, and whoever wrote the best essay will win a trip to Washington, D.C., all expenses paid. I am happy to say, I won (Yay!), and went to D.C. with Diane LaPointe. I went to Washington, D.C. to visit the White House, the Lincoln Memorial and such, and saw a lot of the capital.

I attended a conference and I was on a panel with

other writers. I had to stand up in front of people and talk, and that was something I wasn't good at, but I did it, and it felt great.

NEW ENGLAND HEALTH CARE EMPLOYEES UNION

DISTRICT 1199

AND THE CONNECTICUT NURSING HOMES

T&U

TRAINING & UPGRADING

FUND

Melleta Neil
Certified Nursing Assistant in Training

A Life-Changing Experience

Born and raised in St. Mary, Jamaica, it was always my dream to travel to see other countries and just to understand life from different perspectives.

Back home in Jamaica it was always a struggle to find employments, so it was hard trying to make ends meet. Having to care for three children, I became self-employed. I bought a sewing machine, and I taught myself how to sew. I started to make school uniforms, sheets and drapes. It was a small business, which was slow at times, but it gave me a sense of independence.

The day finally came when I had the opportunity of visiting America with a cousin of mine. I was granted a three-month's visitor's visa. While I was on vacation, my son Renell, who is an American citizen, applied for me to adjust my status. After spending some months waiting to hear, I was finally issued with my permanent resident card ("green card").

This opportunity opened up a new door for me. I am currently in training to become a Certified Nursing Assistant (CNA).

Learning to adjust to the different climates is a new experience for me. It is now October. Summer is gone, and I am getting ready to experience my second winter. This is a life-changing experience, and for me, this is a dream come true.

Kara O'Dwyer
Personal Care Assistant

A Caring Spirit

I came into this world with a caring spirit. Most of my working years have been comprised of jobs which are in service to others. My first degree was an Associate's in Early Childhood and Special Education. I spent years teaching in daycares, camps and after-school programs. In the midst of that career, I became a mom to an amazing boy.

By the time my son was two and a half, I was diagnosed with Lyme Disease. The symptoms changed after double treatments but didn't go away. I took a medical leave, and was then told that I also have fibrobmyalgia. When I learned that my employer no longer had a job for me to go back to, I decided to return to school.

Living with constant pain and fatigue, that caring spirit rose up again in me, insisting that the only way to be healed myself was to help someone else. So I trained to become a massage therapist. It has been a humbling experience bringing healing to my clients. But because my schedule is so unpredictable, I needed something else more stable to supplement my income.

So, just as I was entering my massage career, I met a woman with a disability. We developed a friendship over the course of two years, and I learned that her care team wasn't working well for her any more. I stepped up, along with two of her other friends and someone already in the field. Within a month or so of becoming a PCA, I first learned that homecare workers were able to become part of SEIU/1199. I quickly became involved with as many union events as possible.

Now, two and a half years later, I have been more active than I ever imagined in political action to advance this kind of career, to maintain improvements already made, to protect funding for service, and pretty much anything else which feels like a union issue.

Caring makes me strong, and caring makes my union strong.

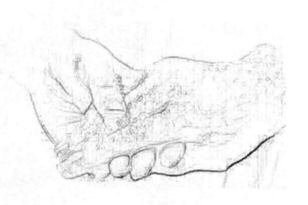

Valentin Otazu-Toro
Saint Mary Home, West Hartford

A Most Beautiful Time

I remember the most beautiful time at work at Saint Mary's Home, a wonderful moment with the residents there.

I am a young and strong handsome male at my union station as I call the attention of my bella resident and they ask me for multiple things to help them. These bella ladies are like an extension of my family, or, more, they are the image of my mother, the beautiful woman who is always in my mind.

I am very happy to attend to everything that they want, especially in the last days of their life. In them, I can see in their eyes everything all the time that my mother did for me from the beginning of her womb, when I was born, when I was growing until I became a man.

I am very happy to be in Saint Mary's house, because it is a time when I can return the love to her, my mother, by this duty to my bella residents, from the bottom of my heart, all the good sacrifices and good things that were offered to me.

141

Aurilia Paiva
Saint Mary Home, West Hartford (Retired)

Stay With Me

This is Helen's and my history.

My name is Aurilia Paiva. I worked in Saint Mary's Home for 38 years. I am retired now. I worked with so many patients. I liked all of them, but I had one favorite patient. Her name was Helen.

After I finished giving care to the other residents in my assignment, I spent a lot of time in Helen's room listening to her life history. I also told her the history of my life.

Helen wanted me to spend time in the night with her, especially when the weather was bad, like snow or rain. She said, "Stay with me, please, don't leave me. Spend your time with me, please...please."

She said, "I love you like a daughter."

Giving love, and receiving love, are the greatest blessings. I was blessed to know Helen and to comfort her when the night was stormy.

Marie "Berline" E. Pauyo
Personal Care Assistant

The Little Maid

I remember when I was a child, my mom had a little child who was doing everything for her as a maid. The little girl had a difficult life, working day and night, with never a day off.

Years later my mom died. I didn't understand what was happening, because I was five years old at the time. But what hurt me the most was when my other family came to pick me up from my mom's house. I saw that little girl in her mom's hand: she was so happy, and now, look at me, what will become of me without my mother?

I think that at the time that my mom was dying, she did not know where I was going to live. The lady who took me away treated me the same way that my mom used to treat her little "maid." It was a very hard time for me, but I survived, just as my mother's "little maid" did.

Now I am a grown woman. I have learned to not treat others the way I would not want to be treated, at work, at school or in someone's home. Treat everyone as if they are a beloved daughter or a son, all of us are deserving of love. All of us are family.

Verna Rodney
St. Camillus Health Center, Stamford

How Did You Sleep?

I met my patient 15 years ago when she came to the facility. She met with an accident when she was in her twenties. She told me she was a nurse and was "Momed" with two sons. But her husband divorced her after the accident and remarried.

She always wants to know about me, so I tell her I'm from the island of Jamaica. She always wants to know about growing up on the island. She even knows a few island words.

Each morning I go in her room. The first thing she says is, "How did you sleep?"

I say, "Good," or sometimes, "Not good."

Then she says, "Which song are we going to sing today?" She *loves* songs from her time, so I always try to go back to the sixties, and we sing together.

One thing that stands out about her is she has good energy. I always joke you can hear her from a mile away. She laughs a lot and tries to tell her funny stories. I try to find out if she is sad sometimes about the accident, because she is still young and living in a facility.

She said, "No, she is happy because things happen in life which we don't have control over. So that teaches me to be grateful for life, things could be worse, and do not take life for granted."

Maribel Rodriguez
Autumn of Buck Hill

Look For a Smile!

One morning Mr. G was just moved from the Laurel wing. I went to introduce myself. I said, "Welcome, my name is Maria. How are you?"

Mr. G. was short and bald and he wore glasses. He was from Italy. I could see he was sad by looking at his face. I said, "So, if you need anything, just let me know."

"He said ok," but with a sorry look.

I left the room feeling very sad for him. I went to the nurse to ask if he was long term or short, and what was his diagnosis. She said the family could not take care of him at home, so he's here for the long term.

Every day I would go in with a smile and say, "Good morning," and I asked, "How are you today" But I would never get a smile, just an "I'm okay."

One day I decided I was going to get a smile out of him, "some way, somehow."

That morning I walked in and I said, "How's my cute old man doing today?"

He paused, looked up and had a surprised look on his face. Then he said, "I'm okay."

I finally asked, "Why are you so sad?"

He said, "My daughter put me here and I can't go see my wife. She's in a nursing home." He explained that his wife had Alzheimer's. He would visit her every day. "Even though she didn't know who I am, and that made me sad, I still visited her and held her hand every day."

I always felt his sadness, but I was intent to make him smile, so I continued to say to him, "How is my cutie-putie today?" Until finally he smiled. And after that day, every day he saw me he would smile! We would talk every day. Little did he know he made *my* day when he would smile.

He was my cutie-putie!

Rose Marie Stanford
Saint Mary Home, West Hartford

A Day To Remember

This is a story of my life and work. The story happened around sixteen years ago. It had very painful moments, but it remains lodged in on my heart.

I was in a very stressful relationship, but going to work would make my day. I worked with an Alzheimer's patient. She came from a wealthy family. We called her, "Sister Nurse" because she had been a nurse in real life. She was very slim and petite. Not a big person at all, but she had a very big heart.

Sister Nurse had one son who put her in a nursing home because he did not have time or could not understand why she was not responding to him in the way he used to know her.

Having children of my own made me understand the pain she was going through, with no love from the family members, especially from her son. He was the only child she had. She still showed love, even though she did not receive it from her son.

One evening before supper, Sister Nurse told me her time had come. She said to me. "I'm going to die."

I told her, "No you're not!"

She replied, "Yes, I am. I'm going to die today!"

I told her, "I'm going outside for your supper and I'm bringing it back in for you."

"She said, "Okay, but I am going to die. Watch me."

I went out to the food cart. It was in the hallway by the door. I removed her tray and carried it back into the room, and as I approached her bed she told me again. "Watch me."

Right after she said, "Watch me," she laid back in the bed, she closed her eyes and she stopped breathing. The look on her face was so peaceful. I knew she was at rest.

I took her hand and held it for a moment because I couldn't believe she was gone. I kept calling to her, but I got no response. I wanted to give her some comfort, but it was too late, Sister Nurse had passed.

I ran outside and called my charge nurse. When I was telling her the story, the nurse was astonished. She hurried into the room to assess the patient. She listened with her stethoscope and felt for a pulse, but there was no sign of life.

We all said, "She is smiling, she looks very peaceful and calm."

It was all terribly sad, and very unbelievable that someone would say they were going to pass on, and they did.

I was very traumatized, because I looked forward to spending time with Sister Nurse, as we called her. Going to her room and seeing Sister Nurse lying in bed was very, very sad. Sister Nurse was loved by the staff of the nursing home. Wow, that was a day to remember in my book.

NEW ENGLAND HEALTH CARE EMPLOYEES UNION

DISTRICT 1199

AND THE CONNECTICUT NURSING HOMES

T&U

TRAINING & UPGRADING

FUND

Gloria Stewart

Dementia of People We Love

I am a CNA, and I graduated from the Capital Community College. After graduation, I was successful in obtaining a job at one of our nursing homes in the Hartford, Connecticut area.

I was hired to work on the 11-7 AM shift. I was happy and grateful that I was able to get the job, where I could earn a living and enjoy a better life,

There were patients who were very sick with dementia. They needed the help of someone to take care of them whom they knew very well.

There was one patient who knew me very well. Because of the tone of my voice and my gentle hands, we became good friends. I will call him Mister Smith. He was of tall stature and of slim build, which made it easier for me to handle him and take care of him. He had a full head of hair, and he even had hairy ears.

One evening when I came on to start my shift, I wore a different hairstyle than the one I usually had. Mr. Smith had never seen me wearing this style before. He became very angry when he saw me and began hitting me. He did not say anything, he just hit me, right in the face. It was very painful.

I called his name and said, "Mr. Smith, why do you hit me?" He did not say anything, he just kept hitting me. I could not understand why he was acting so violently.

After I came out of the room I made a report to the nurse. She said that probably I had been rough with him, which was not true, I am always gentle with my patients

But after thinking about it I realized he had not recognized me because of the change of my hairstyle. I seemed like a different person to him. From that day on, I never changed my hairstyle until after his death.

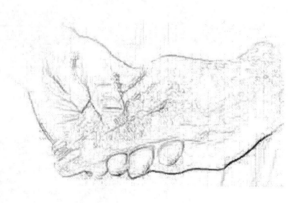

Norma Wallace
Autumn Lake Healthcare at New Britain

Waking From a Coma

My name is Norma Wallace. A few years ago I was pregnant. I was visiting my mother and I hit my toe on a stone. A day later I noticed the baby wasn't moving in my belly, so I went to the doctor.

After a week went by, the doctor induced my labor and the baby, a little boy, was born. But the baby had died. We were going to name him Roy, Jr. after his father.

Shortly after the baby was born I went into renal failure (kidney failure). I fell into a coma and the doctor pronounced me 'dead'.

The nurses covered me up with white sheets. They were about to take me to the morgue.

While I was laying in the room waiting for them to come and take me, a young Cuban doctor who was not on duty came into my room. The doctor took hold of my hand. He started screaming. He said, "This girl is not dead, she is still ALIVE!"

Soon after that I opened my eyes and looked at the young doctor. He was almost as confused as me. He said, "I don't know what led me to come into your room today, you are not even my patient."

To this day, I do not know what made the Cuban doctor come into my room and check on me. But something brought him to me. And here I am today. I give thanks unto God for saving my life, and now I am a certified nursing assistant trying to help people who need a little help.

Refila Walters
Maple View Manor, Rocky Hill

Growing Up With My Grandparents

When I was a little girl growing up in Jamaica with my grandparents, they raised cows, goats, pigs and chickens. In the morning we as the grandkids would have to do and collect the eggs from the chicken coop and feed them before we went off to school.

One morning my cousin and I went to get the eggs, but the rooster would not let us into the coop. So we put some corn in the feed pan. He moved over a little, along with some of the hens, so we were able to get to the eggs.

But the rooster came back toward us. He was in front of the door, and he attacked us with his talons. There was blood all over us where he scratched us. We started to cry and we called for help. When my grandfather came running, he had a difficult time to get in to help us. He needed help to save himself, too!

Grandfather was in the coop with us, he was trying to save us, when the other rooster started to attack us. Our uncle came running, he heard all the cries for help. Uncle cut a hole in the wire fence and helped us squeeze through the fence to get away from the roosters.

No one had any eggs for breakfast that morning.

I loved growing up with my grandmother and grandfather and my uncle and aunt. I feel those were the best years of my life, in the country. We had a lot of work, but it was fun (except when we were attacked by rooster). They spoiled us grandchildren. At times I would say, if things could change, I would live my life all over again with them on the farm. But they are no longer with us. I miss them so much.

Most chickens are very nice animals, but that rooster was just mean.

TITLES FROM HARD BALL PRESS

Winning Richmond: How a Progressive Alliance Won City Hall – by Gayle McLaughlin

A Great Vision – A Militant Family's Journey Through the Twentieth Century – by Richard March

Caring – 1199 Nursing Home Workers Tell Their Story

Fight For Your Long Day – Classroom Edition, by Alex Kudera

Love Dies, a thriller, by Timothy Sheard

Murder of a Post Office Manager, A Legal Thriller, by Paul Felton

New York Hustle – Pool Rooms, School Rooms and Street Corners, a memoir, Stan Maron

Passion's Pride – Return to the Dawning, Cathie Wright- Lewis

The Secrets of the Snow, a book of poetry, Hiva Panahi

Sixteen Tons, a Novel, by Kevin Corley

Throw Out the Water, the sequel to Sixteen Tons, by Kevin Corley

We Are One – Stories of Work, Life & Love, Elizabeth Gottieb (editor)

What Did You Learn at Work Today? The Forbidden Lessons of Labor Education, by Helena Worthen

With Our Loving Hands – 1199 Nursing Home Workers Tell Their Story

Winning Richmond – How a Progressive Alliance Won City Hall, by Gayle McLaughlin

Woman Missing, A Mill Town Mystery, by Linda Nordquist

THE LENNY MOSS MYSTERIES by Timothy Sheard

This Won't Hurt A Bit

Some Cuts Never Heal

A Race Against Death

No Place To Be Sick

Slim To None

A Bitter Pill

Someone Has To Die

HARD BALL PRESS CHILDREN'S BOOKS

The Cabbage That Came Back, Stephen Pearl (author), Rafael Pearl (Illustrator), Sara Pearl (translator)

Good Guy Jake, Mark Torres (author), Yana Podrieez (Illustrator), Madelin Arroyo (translator)

Hats Off For Gabbie, Marivir Montebon (author), Yana Podriez (illustrator), Madelin Arroyo (translator)

Jimmy's Carwash Adventure, Victor Narro (author & translator), Yana Podriez (illustrator)

Joelito's Big Decision, Ann Berlak (author), Daniel Camacho (Illustrator), José Antonio Galloso (Translator)

Manny & The Mango Tree, Ali R. Bustamante (author), Monica Lunot-Kuker (illustrator), Mauricio Niebla (translator)

Margarito's Forest, Andy Carter (author), Allison Havens (illustrator), Omar Mejia (Translator)

Polar Bear Pete's Ice is Melting! – Timothy Sheard (author), Madelin Arroyo (translator), A FALL 2018 RELEASE

Trailer Park – Jennifer Dillard (author), Madelin Arroyo (translator), Rafael Pearl (illustrator) A SUMMER